MODERN DRUM SET
STICKINGS

by Swiss Chris

Illustration by
Lakecia Davis-Flueck

Speed • Pitch • Balance • Loop

To access audio visit:
www.halleonard.com/mylibrary

Enter Code
6808-1992-2883-3678

ISBN 978-1-60378-132-9

Copyright © 2012 Cherry Lane Music Company
International Copyright Secured   All Rights Reserved

No part of this publication may be reproduced in any form or by
any means without the prior written permission of the Publisher.

Visit Hal Leonard Online at
www.halleonard.com

Contact us:
Hal Leonard
7777 West Bluemound Road
Milwaukee, WI 53213
Email: info@halleonard.com

In Europe, contact:
Hal Leonard Europe Limited
42 Wigmore Street
Marylebone, London, W1U 2RN
Email: info@halleonardeurope.com

In Australia, contact:
Hal Leonard Australia Pty. Ltd.
4 Lentara Court
Cheltenham, Victoria, 3192 Australia
Email: info@halleonard.com.au

CONTENTS

FOREWORD by Skip Hadden

This book provides a unique opportunity for drummers to realize and build on several concepts within its covers. Many drum books are about specific styles and beats. This one is about the nuts and bolts of our instrument and craft. It presents the foundation of drumming and how we can unlock that foundation to make our playing both more concrete and more musical.

For example, his use of the basic building blocks of rhythm, the groups of two's and three's that make up phrases in the duple and triplet meters. His musical checklist to move us into the realm of form and phrasing, and how to develop them, and the audio tracks of his playing to support what's on the written page, all point to the path of excellence. All these steps lead to forming a concept with which, through playing simple ideas with the utmost musical intent, a path to success can be realized.

This book is written by a unique individual, "Swiss" Chris Flueck. Reading through his bio and the long list of who he's performed and recorded with provides us with some degree of information regarding what he has accomplished in his substantial career, but it provides little in letting us know of the depth of his commitment and understanding of music and drumming. It also doesn't give us any idea of what he had to do to get to where he is.

I have had the honor to be in a front row seat at the unfolding of this amazing young man's development. He was a student at Berklee College of Music from 1991 to 1996. He arrived possessing strong basic skills and some practical performance experience. He built on these strong fundamental skills and was quickly rewarded with scholarship support as "The Most Improved Drummer" at the time. He continued to build on this success and, with his infectious energy, drive, and playing skills, finished his academic career playing every possible musical setting imaginable.

He took that determination, that drive, that commitment, and that focus out into the world and never saw a challenge that slowed him down. All situations before him presented possibilities to grow and learn. Now with this book he finds himself in a position where he can share some of that experience and knowledge with all who are interested in their own awareness of what is possible for them, and pursue a path to achieve it.

Welcome to a world of possibilities via "Swiss" Chris!

CHRIS'S SETUP

NATAL
1. 20 x 18 Kick
2. 10 x 6.5 Tom
3. 12 x 7 Tom
4. 14 x 12 Floor Tom
5. 16 x14 Floor Tom
6. 13 x 7 Snare
7. 14 x 5.5 Snare

ROLAND
8. 2x SPD-SX pads

SABIAN
(different options depending on the gig)
a. 2 Rides (El Sabor or Omni)
b. 4 Crashes (HHX or AAX)
c. 2 Hi-Hats (regular and x-hat) (HHX or AAX)

JCR Percussion - Bronx
d. 3 Cowbells
   - Low to the left
   - High to the right
   - another cowbell, low or high in the middle

EVANS
Drumheads

REGAL TIP
Sticks

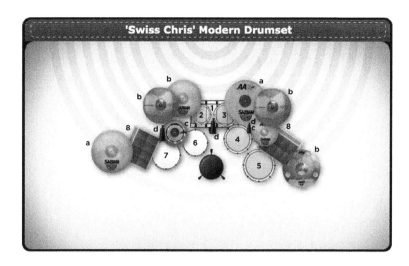
'Swiss Chris' Modern Drumset

DRUM SET KEY

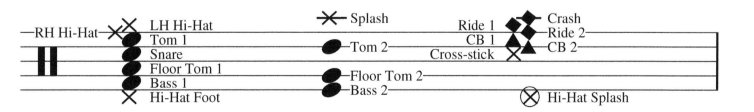

HOW TO USE THE TOOLS IN THIS BOOK

Working with this book, you can create your own funk, soul, swing, blues, rock, blast beat, Afro-pop, disco-funk, hip-hop (Old and New School), southern bounce, reggae, dance hall, Afro-Cuban, Brazilian, Haitian, West Indies, African, etc. grooves.

You can also use the sticking pages found on pages 71–72 as a tool to solo and write percussion pieces.

Always check/cross-reference the Musical Checklist (The Seven Principles, page 12) while working on the sticking matrices and their applications or any other reading chart.

Choose: a) a sticking from one of the Sticking Matrices (pages 27–29) and **b)** a Sticking Page Application (Chapter 7), and move through all of the principles on the Musical Checklist (page 12 and below).

Identify the following points:

1. Melody
2. Pulse
3. Subdivision
4. Sticking
5. Orchestration
6. Dynamics
7. Resolution Points

Have fun with it …

CHAPTER 1
Mental Aspects of Drumming
Ask, Believe, Receive

Through repetitive exposure using the materials in this book—the Duplet and Triplet Matrices, the Musical Checklist, and the Sticking Page Applications—you will grow quickly.

Visualize yourself orchestrating the stickings on the drums before you practice.

Take three long deep breaths before you start playing, get into a zone, and feel good.

Always remember:

- Sing the sticking melodies.
- Count out loud while you are playing the stickings.
- Play the stickings two ways: straight and swung.
- Use the Singing/Beatbox Concept (The Boo-Ts-Ki-Ts Method).

Practice all sticking exercises from slow to fast and fast to slow, and from super soft (***ppp***) to super loud (***fff***) and then back to super soft (***ppp***); do these with both right hand and left hand lead. Perform each sticking line eight times to penetrate your conscious mind and reach the subconscious mind.

Enjoy the ride, have fun with the process, and remember: you are only competing with yourself.

Remember to play with the *attitude of gratitude.*

Believe positively about yourself and enjoy drums and drumming.

"Whatever we think and thank about, we bring about."

Swiss Chris with the NATAL TEAM in Frankfurt, 2011

CHAPTER 2
Physical Aspects of Drumming

Knowledge of and a command of the following points make a drummer a more complete musician:

- Selection of drumsticks and practice pad
- Brief history about rudiments
- Basic hand/foot techniques
  (Traditional and matched grips/formal and informal movements/Free stroke and Moeller stroke)
- Stickings in duplet and triplet meter
- The Sticking Page Applications
- Reading/Interpretation (Melodic Accent Control Charts)
- Timekeeping (Musical Checklist and Sticking Matrices)
- Styles: funk, soul, R&B, hip-hop, reggae, jazz, blues, Latin, Cuban, Brazilian, Haitian, Afro-pop, and traditional African styles
- Accuracy/Precision
- Identity—personal style
- Musicality (Musical Checklist/Swiss's recommendations)

These aspects all work together.

I believe that the mental aspect of drumming/performing must be considered first, because if you don't have a mental grasp on musical concepts, you cannot manifest the concepts correctly in the physical realm.

Clear speech is the product of clear thought: *"Say it, sing it, play it."*

 TRACK 1: Intro Freestyle in Duplet Meter

TRACK 2: Intro Freestyle in Triplet Meter

SELECTION OF DRUMSTICKS

Each drummer must find the right sticks, brushes, and mallets that work for him or her. The evaluation process of getting the right pair of drumsticks depends on the size, weight, levelness, and balance of the sticks.

Checklist for drumsticks:

Size	The size depends on the hand size of the student (small hand = small stick, etc.).
Weight	Turn your wrist from side to side—you have to feel comfortable, and both sticks have to weigh the same.
Levelness	Roll the sticks on an even counter. If the stick "wobbles," do not use it.
Balance	Bounce the stick on a surface such as the floor or a table, holding the stick at the fulcrum with the thumb and index finger. Balancing the stick, feel the rebound.

SELECTION OF PRACTICE PAD

- Soft rubber pad for quiet practice
- Hard rubber pad for intensifying the workout and hearing each stroke
- Double surface practice pad for different sounds

Tip: Check out the Corpmaster ScoJo Scott Johnson stick. It has a rubber tip, and you can warm up on any surface. It is a practice pad and a stick in one.

A BRIEF HISTORY OF RUDIMENTS

Definition: "Rudiments" comes from the Latin word "rudis," which was a wooden practice sword used by gladiators. Rudiments are some of the basic building blocks or patterns used in drumming vocabulary and can be combined in a great variety of ways.

Tip: Most of the stickings on the duplet and triplet matrices are also rudiments.

When I was in the fifth grade, as a part of a history lesson presentation, I chose to do a report on the history of my first love: the field drum. Here is a brief history, starting in my homeland of Switzerland:

On a hot summer day on July 9, 1386, at the Battle of Sempach, Luzern, the Swiss troops were successfully defending themselves from the "Habsburger" (The Austrian/German Empire). They increasingly used drums and fifes to signal the troops in battle. Their drums and fifes signaling system spread throughout Europe, since the Swiss troops were deployed as mercenaries in Western Europe.

The first rudimental publication, *Orchesographie*, came from Dijon, France, by Thoinot Arbeau in 1588. The publication included Swiss rudiments. Also, the first written rudiments go back to the beginning of the 1600s in Basel, Switzerland. I can prove that, as a student of Jakob Otter from the Tambourenverein Laupersdorf-Thal, sources are always mentioning the importance of the Swiss Basler trommeln. We studied and always honored the Basler trommeln (probably the highest level of all). The birthplace of rudimental drumming is said to be France since, in the 17th and 18th centuries, pro drummers became part of the King's honor guard. During the rule of Napoleon I, the craft was perfected. The march, "Le Rigodon," and its different interpretations in the 18th century, is still one of the cornerstones of modern rudimental drumming. But let's not forget Scottish pipe drumming and American drumming. (I also think that the Americans are always taking it to the next level.)

America's first published basic rudiments came via Baron Friedrich von Steuben. Outlining drum signals for the revolutionary troops, his book *Regulations for the Order and Discipline of the Troops of the United States* was published in 1779. Although they were not exactly rudiments, the development was clear.

Known as the Father of Rudimental Drumming, Charles Stewart Ashworth is said to have originated the concept of rudiments. His 1812 book probably has the longest title of any drum publication ever: *A New, Useful and Complete System of Drum Beating Including the Reveille, Troop, Retreat, Officer's Calls, Signals, Salutes and the Whole of the Camp Duty as Practiced at Head Quarters, Washington City; Intended Particularly for the United States Army and Navy...* Wow... what a title.

Here are some of my favorite books connecting rudiments to drum set playing and applications. This list is by no means complete—these are some classic titles that are also personal favorites that help delineate some of the modern trends of rudimental development:

1935	*Stick Control* (George Lawrence Stone)	
1938	*Gene Krupa Drum Method* (Gene Krupa)	
1941	*Modern Rudimental Swing Solos for the Advanced Drummer* (Charley Wilcoxon)	
1942	*Buddy Rich's Modern Interpretation of Snare Drum Rudiments* (Buddy Rich and Henry Adler)	
1983	*Master Studies* (Joe Morello)	
1996	*It's Your Move* (Dom Famularo w/Joe Bergamini)	
1997	*The Drummer's Complete Vocabulary as Taught by Alan Dawson* (Alan Dawson/John Ramsay)	
1998	*The Complete Drumset Rudiments* (Peter Magadini)	
2000	*Rudimental Logic* (Bill Bachman)	

Please research and recognize the following drum teacher lineage:

- **Billy Gladstone** (Techniques) taught Joe Morello, Ted Reed, Morris "Arnie" Lang
- **George Lawrence Stone** (Free Stroke) taught Joe Morello, Vic Firth
- **Sanford A. Moeller** (Moeller Stroke) taught Jim Chapin

All three influenced Dom Famularo's Range of Motion (Hands & Feet).

All of the above teachers have a direct or indirect influence on today's contemporary drumming style.

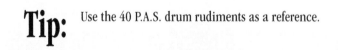

Tip: Use the 40 P.A.S. drum rudiments as a reference.

BASIC HAND/FOOT TECHNIQUES

Hand Technique

Since we are considering an ambidextrous approach to playing—leading with either the right or the left hand—I recommend playing in a matched grip; that is, both hands are holding the stick at the fulcrum, between the flat part of the thumb and the first joint of the index finger, with the other three fingers wrapped loosely, not squeezing, around the stick.

 Tip: Check out the following books and DVDs:

It's Your Move by Dom Famularo (Book)

Speed, Power, Control, Endurance by Jim Chapin (DVD)

The Next Level—Rudimental Snare Drum Techniques by Jeff Queen (Book)

Playing with Sticks by Jeff Queen (DVD)

Secret Weapons for the Modern Drummer by Jojo Mayer (DVD)

Foot Technique

I recommend both heel-down and heel-up playing, depending on the musical situation.

 Tip: Play everything with your feet as you play with your hands, then later match them in unison. Colin Bailey's *Bass Drum Control* is a great book. Also, *Pedal Control* by Dom Famularo and Joe Bergamini is a must for the serious teacher/player.

Tip: Consult your private drum teacher about other methods… there is not only one way to play follow your heart… evaluate… don't settle for the first approach… make sure it feels good to you… always start slow and always stay relaxed.

CHAPTER 3
Musical Checklist (The Seven Principles)

I use the following musical checklist in almost every musical situation. This is one of the most important tools for infinite growth through music.

This musical checklist will guide you through a series of decisions that will allow you to have total control of your instrument. By getting into the habit of thinking about all seven points each time you play the drums, it will allow you to excel with total knowledge and total awareness of what you are doing on your instrument.

1. Melody
2. Pulse
3. Subdivision
4. Sticking
5. Orchestration
6. Dynamics
7. Resolution Points

The following explanations are meant as a guide to help you understand the scope and meaning of each term on the checklist, followed by a set of guidelines to help you zoom in and focus on separating each element and practicing it individually.

1. MELODY

Being able to sing what you play is the first step. If you can't sing it, then it is a sign that the musical concept is not internalized. This is a fun and simple way to begin practicing with an organized concept for singing.

Hear melodies, recognize them, appreciate them, sing them, and then play them. Have fun. Let us say: "You are the drum, the first telephone. The first people were storytellers, les griots, MCs, poets, and singers. The word has to be heard!!!"

Swiss Drum Beat Syllables—The Singing/Beatbox Concept (The Boo-Ts-Ki-Ts Method)

"Say it, Sing it, Play it!"

Use these syllables as the building blocks to start constructing and building your beats like songs (melodies), using your voice as the first step in understanding what you are about to learn to play on the drums with sticks.

SOUND SOURCE	SYLLABLES	NOTATION
Kick	Boo or Boom	Quarter Note
	Bo-Go	Eighth Notes
Snare	Ka or Kat/Ki or Kit	Quarter Note
	Ka-Ta or Ki-Ti	Eighth Notes
Snare Flam	Klat	Quarter Note
	Klat-Klat	Eighth Notes
Hi-Hat Closed	T	Quarter Note
	T-T	Eighth Notes
Hi-Hat Half Open	Ts	Quarter Note
	Ts-Ts	Eighth Notes
Hi-Hat Open	Tsch	Quarter Note
	Tsch-Tsch	Eighth Notes
Small Tom	Tim	Quarter Note
	Ti-Gi	Eighth Notes
Medium Tom	Tam	Quarter Note
	Ta-Ga	Eighth Notes
Floor Tom	Tum	Quarter Note
	Tu-Gu	Eighth Notes
High Cowbell	Bling	Quarter Note
	Bling-Bling	Eighth Notes
Low Cowbell	Blong	Quarter Note
	Blong-Blong	Eighth Notes
Ride Cymbal	Ching	Quarter Note
	Ching-A (uh)	Eighth Notes
Crashes	Psch	Quarter Note
	Psch-Psch	Eighth Notes

Here is an example of a way to create a beat out of the syllables with an alternating single stroke sticking RLRL. Apply the first "R" on the bass drum (Boo or Boom); the first "L" on the hi-hat half open (Ts); the second "R" on the snare (Ka or Ki); and the second "L" on the hi-hat half open (Ts). (This application of one limb at a time is a linear beat.)

Sing this out loud:

Boo	Ts	Ki	Ts	Boo	Ts	Ki	Ts
RF	LH	RH	LH	RF	LH	RH	LH

TRACK 3: Melody Syllables

TRACK 4: Boo-Ts-Ki-Ts Melody

TRACK 5: Boo-Ts-Ki-Ts Melody, Slowly Then Fast

"Swiss Chris with legendary beatboxer/human orchestra Kenny Muhammad"

"Swiss Chris with Berklee faculty member Alonzo Harris and the legendary beatboxer Rahzel"

2. PULSE

Pulse is a regular, recurring emphasis of a fixed interval of time. Much like we feel our heart beat in a regular pulse, we often feel a regular beat, or pulse, in music.

 TRACK 6: Heartbeat Sample

In some musical cases, the pulse and the kick drum are identical or close to identical. In jazz/ swing music of the 1920s and '30s, the bass drum drove the music. The bass drum also drives the parade. When you go watch a parade, what do you hear first? The bass drums. Likewise, in a samba/batucada group, the surdo (low, mostly double-headed drum) drives the spirit of the Carnival in Brazil.

Check out the kick drum sound (Boo or Boom). The focus here is on the pulsation of the bass drum and how it drives the song. There is no backbeat on 2 and 4 for the following examples:

 TRACK 7: Four on the Floor

Disco-Funk (Four on the floor)
Boo-Ts- Boo-Ts- Boo-Ts- Boo-Ts   (Repeat)
>   >   >   >   (Quarter Note Accent)

 TRACK 8: Shuffle the Blues

Shuffle/Blues (Basic sticking in triplet meter matrix)
Boo-(Ki)-Boo- Boo-(Ki)-Boo- Boo-(Ki)-Boo- Boo-(Ki)-Boo   (Repeat)
>   >   >   >   (Dotted Quarter Note Accent)

TRACK 9: Samba Foot Action

Brazilian/Samba/Funk Bass Drum Part
Boo-Ki-Ti-Boo-Boo-Ki-Ti-Boo-Boo-Ki-Ti-Boo-Boo-Ki-Ti-Boo   (Repeat)
>   >   >   >   (Quarter Note Accent)

3. SUBDIVISION

Beats are subdivided into smaller parts—in our case 2, 3, 4, 6, 8, 12, 16, 24, 32, 48, or 64 even parts—in either duplet or triplet subdivision. Even those rhythms can be played either straight or shuffled.

 TRACK 10: Straight Eighth Notes, Then Swinging Eighth Notes

Straight eighth notes:

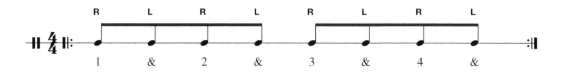

Count out loud.

Swinging eighth notes:

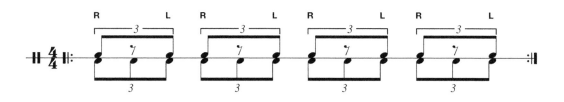

Shuffle construction:

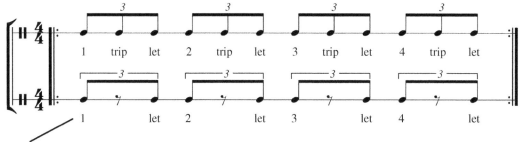

Only play and sing the first and last partial of the triplet.

Counting Subdivisions

 TRACK 11: Quarter Note Count

Quarter note subdivision with quarter note pulse:

Eighth note subdivision with quarter note pulse:

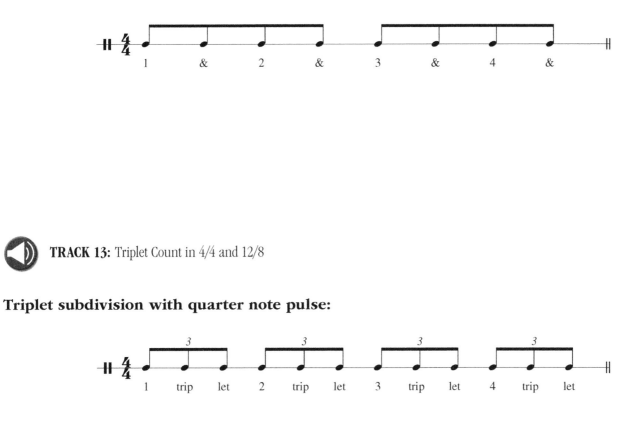

Triplet subdivision with quarter note pulse:

Triplet subdivision with dotted quarter note pulse:

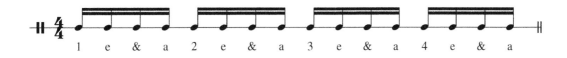

16th note subdivision with quarter note pulse:

TRACK 15: Sextuplet Count (3 x 2) in 4/4 and 12/8

Sextuplet subdivision with quarter note pulse:

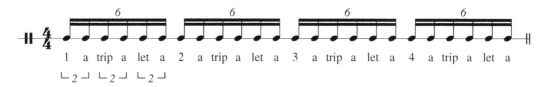

Sextuplet subdivision with dotted quarter note pulse:

 TRACK 16: 12/8 Count (2 x 3)

 TRACK 17: 32nd Note Count

32nd note subdivision with quarter note pulse:

 TRACK 18: Drum Solo While Counting 16th Notes

4. STICKING

Play the following basic stickings from slow to fast and fast to slow:

1.	Single Stroke Roll	**RL** or **LR**
2.	Double Stroke Roll	**RRLL** or **LLRR**
3.	Triple Stroke Roll	**RRR LLL** or **LLL RRR**
4.	Quadruple Stroke Roll	**RRRR LLLL** or **LLLL RRRR**
5.	Single Paradiddle	**RLRR LRLL** or **LRLL RLRR***
6.	Double Paradiddle	**RLRLRR LRLRLL***
7.	Triple Paradiddle	**RLRLRLRR LRLRLRLL***
8.	Single Paradiddle-diddle	**RLRRLL** or **LRLLRR***
9.	Double Paradiddle-diddle	**RLRLRRLL** or **LRLRLLRR***
10.	Six Stroke Roll	**RLLRRL** or **LRRLLR***

(***Note**: Also play stickings 5–10 starting with the LH, and for example 5, play all of the Single Paradiddle permutation possibilities below.)

TRACK 19: Single Stroke Roll

TRACK 20: Double Stroke Roll (from half notes to more than 32nd triplets and back)

TRACK 21: Triple Stroke Roll (double hi-hat 3 against 2 foot ostinato)

TRACK 22: Quadruple Stroke Roll

TRACK 23: Single Paradiddle

TRACK 24: Double Paradiddle

TRACK 25: Triple Paradiddle

TRACK 26: Single Paradiddle-Diddle (example derived from Haitian "Nago" rhythm)

TRACK 27: Double Paradiddle-Diddle

TRACK 28: Six Stroke Roll

Permutations for Example 5, the Single Paradiddle

A permutation is simply an ordered arrangement of the elements of a set. In notation, one can arrange the "natural" ordering of the elements being permuted in a row; in our case, we are moving the stickings bit by bit to the left. Thus, all of the stickings under the Paradiddle are permutations.

Single Paradiddle	**RLRR**	**LRLL**
	LRRL	RLLR
	RRLR	LLRL
	RLRL	LRLR
	LRLL	RLRR
	RLLR	LRRL
	LLRL	RRLR
	LRLR	RLRL

All abovementioned Single Paradiddle sticking permutations are included in our duplet meter sticking matrix on page 71.

5. ORCHESTRATION

Orchestration on the drums refers to using different sound sources in a melodic or harmonic way. Where do we orchestrate the sticking melody on the drums?

On the ride cymbal, cowbell, toms, snare, hi-hat, and bass drum, etc.

Expand your creative potential by interchanging the following orchestration options into your exercises:

- Using sticks, mallets, brushes, or fingers
- Turning snare(s) on or off
- Playing in the middle or on the edge of the drumhead
- Playing on the shell of any drum
- Playing on the hardware (hi-hat or cymbal stand)
- Playing on the rim of any drum
- Playing into the drums or using rebound (hands and feet)
- Playing in the air (air drumming)
- Making various cymbal orchestration decisions:
    - a. on the bell of the cymbal
    - b. in the middle of the cymbal
    - c. on the edge of the cymbal
    - d. "choking" the cymbal

Tip: Have fun and experience infinite orchestration possibilities.

 TRACK 29: Drum Orchestration Solo

6. DYNAMICS

In music, dynamics refer to both the volume of a note and the execution of a piece, such as staccato and legato, etc.

ppp	**pianississimo**	"very, very soft"
pp	**pianissimo**	"very soft"
p	**piano**	"soft"
mp	**mezzo-piano**	"moderately soft"
mf	**mezzo-forte**	"moderately loud"
f	**forte**	"loud" or "strong"
ff	**fortissimo**	"very loud"
fff	**fortississimo**	"very, very loud" or "super loud"

Decrescendo (⟩): Gradually getting softer

Crescendo (⟨): Gradually getting louder

Accent (>): Louder stroke

Playing triplets with decrescendos creates the illusion of a delay effect in dub style music.

 TRACK 30: Delay Effect Dub-Style

Naturally, there will be more than three sound levels in a real-world musical situation. But for our purposes with the stickings in duplet and triplet meter, we will be using a three-sound level concept:

p   non-accented notes on snare drum and hi-hat

mf   accented notes on the hi-hat with shoulder of a stick

f   accented notes on the bass drum and snare drum

 TRACK 31: Three-Sound Level Concept

7. RESOLUTION POINTS

Resolution points are strong musical accents to resolve a phrase. In big band terms, they are called ensemble figures. Think like a horn player … Have fun with the musical accents (i.e., resolution points). Breathe … Sing out loud … Enjoy …

Play the following melodic charts and exercises with resolution points. Sing the melody bar by bar and line by line. Count out loud and tap the melody line in the following ways:

   a.   RH

   b.   LH

   c.   RF

   d.   LF

   e.   All limbs together

Eighth Note Resolution Points

(Can be played in straight or swinging eighth notes.)

 TRACK 32: Eighth Note Resolution Points, Straight

TRACK 33: Eighth Note Resolution Points, Swinging

TRACK 34: Eighth Note Triplet Chart

16th Note Exercises

(Can be played in straight or swinging 16th notes.)

 TRACK 35: 16th Note Chart, Straight

TRACK 36: 16th Note Chart, Swinging

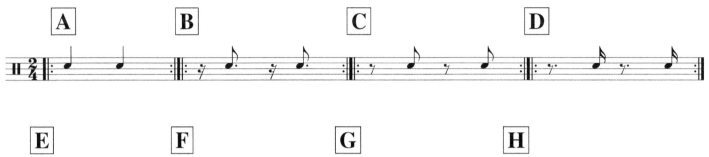

6/8 Exercises

TRACK 37: 6/8 Accent Note Chart

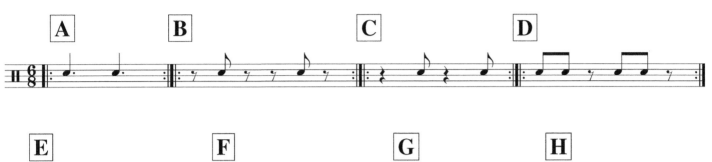

CHAPTER 4

The Official Swiss Chris Warm-Up Exercises

Play all limbs in unison (at the same time):

 TRACK 38: Warm-Up, Triplets

1. One Trip Let

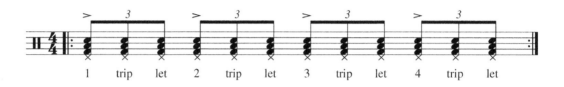

 TRACK 38: Warm-Up, Sextuplets

2. One A Trip A Let A

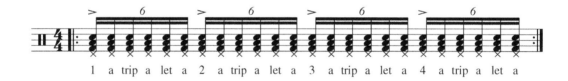

 TRACK 38: Warm-Up, 16ths

3. One E And A

Tip: Please feel free to come up with your own names/phrases. Simply count the syllables and create your own Unison Warm-Up. Use your name and play it as your own mantra. For example, Art Blakey would be 3; Kenwood Dennard would be 4; David Garibaldi would be 6, etc.

CHAPTER 5
Sticking Matrix in Duplet Meter
(Binary Rhythm)

Memorize and practice these 32 stickings. They are the basis of this book and will be applied in a multitude of ways in the ensuing chapters. In **1R**, you will begin the sticking with your **right hand**. In **1L**, you begin the sticking with your **left hand**.

STICKING NUMBER	16th Note Count				TITLE
	1 e & a	2 e & a	3 e & a	4 e & a	
	32nd Note Count				
	1 e did a	& a did a	2 e did a	& a did a	
1R	R R R R	L L L L	R R R R	L L L L	Power of 4
1L	L L L L	R R R R	L L L L	R R R R	
2R	R L R L	R L R L	R L R L	R L R L	Singles
2L	L R L R	L R L R	L R L R	L R L R	
3R	R R L L	R R L L	R R L L	R R L L	Doubles
3L	L L R R	L L R R	L L R R	L L R R	
4R	R L L R	R L L R	R L L R	R L L R	Inverted Doubles
4L	L R R L	L R R L	L R R L	L R R L	
5R	R L R R	L R L L	R L R R	L R L L	Paradiddle
5L	L R L L	R L R R	L R L L	R L R R	
6R	R L L R	L R R L	R L L R	L R R L	Paradiddle Permutation-PP1
6L	L R R L	R L L R	L R R L	R L L R	
7R	R R L R	L L R L	R R L R	L L R L	PP2
7L	L L R L	R R L R	L L R L	R R L R	
8R	R L R L	L R L R	R L R L	L R L R	PP3
8L	L R L R	R L R L	L R L R	R L R L	
9R	R L R L	R L R R	L R L R	L R L L	Triple Paradiddle
9L	L R L R	L R L L	R L R L	R L R R	
10R	R L R R	L R R L	R L R R	L R R L	Swiss Bounce
10L	L R L L	R L L R	L R L L	R L L R	
11R	R L L R	L L L R	L L R L	R L L L	Rumba Clave 3:2
11L	L R R L	R R R L	R R L R	L R R R	
12R	R L L R	L L R L	L R L L	R L R L	Dance Hall 1
12L	L R R L	R R L R	R L R R	L R L R	
13R	R L L R	L L R L	R L L R	L L R L	Dance Hall 2
13L	L R R L	R R L R	L R R L	R R L R	
14R	R L R R	L L R L	R R L L	R L R R	J. Chapin (X1)
14L	L R L L	R R L R	L L R R	L R L L	
15R	R L L R	L L R L	L R L L	R L R R	J. Chapin (X2)
15L	L R R L	R R L R	R L R R	L R L L	
16R	R L R R	R R L R	L L L L	R L R R	J. Chapin (X3)
16L	L R L L	L L R L	R R R R	L R L L	

(Numbers 14–16 [X1–3] are cross-rhythms dedicated to the late, great Jim Chapin.)

The sticking matrices can be visualized, memorized, and practiced with infinite possibilities. For example: just hands, just feet, RH and LF, RF and LH, etc.

All of the exercises should serve as an inspiration for people to use the Sticking Matrix in Duplet Meter, the Sticking Matrix in Triplet Meter, and the Musical Checklist to make up their own exercises. The repetitions of an exercise can be decided by the students' or teachers' timetable.

The cells in the Sticking Matrix in Duplet Meter and the Sticking Matrix in Triplet Meter can be read in the following ways:

- horizontally
- vertically
- diagonally

CHAPTER 6
Sticking Matrix in Triplet Meter (Ternary Rhythm)

Again, memorize and practice these stickings as they are the basis of this book, and will be applied in a multitude of ways in the ensuing chapters. In **1R**, you will begin the sticking with your **right hand**. In **1L**, you begin the sticking with your **left hand**.

STICKING NUMBER	Eighth Note Triplet Count												TITLE
	1 trip let			**2** trip let			**3** trip let			**4** trip let			
	16th Note Triplet Count												
	1 a trip			a let a			**2** a trip			a let a			
	1 trip let			**&** trip let			**2** trip let			**&** trip let			
1R	R	R	R	L	L	L	R	R	R	L	L	L	Power of 3
1L	L	L	L	R	R	R	L	L	L	R	R	R	
2R	R	L	R	L	R	L	R	L	R	L	R	L	Singles
2L	L	R	L	R	L	R	L	R	L	R	L	R	
3R	R	R	L	L	R	R	L	L	R	R	L	L	Doubles (X)*
3L	L	L	R	R	L	L	R	R	L	L	R	R	
4R	R	L	R	R	L	R	R	L	R	R	L	R	Shuffle
4L	L	R	L	L	R	L	L	R	L	L	R	L	
5R	R	L	L	R	L	L	R	L	L	R	L	L	Open Drag
5L	L	R	R	L	R	R	L	R	R	L	R	R	
6R	R	L	R	L	L	R	L	R	L	R	L	L	Afro-Cuban 6/8 Clave
6L	L	R	L	R	R	L	R	L	R	L	R	R	
7R	R	L	R	L	R	R	L	R	L	R	L	R	Afro-Cuban 6/8 Bell
7L	L	R	L	R	L	L	R	L	R	L	R	L	
8R	R	L	R	R	L	L	R	L	R	R	L	L	Nago**
8L	L	R	L	L	R	R	L	R	L	L	R	R	
9R	R	L	R	L	R	L	R	R	L	R	L	R	Yanvalou***
9L	L	R	L	R	L	R	L	L	R	L	R	L	
10R	R	L	L	R	L	R	R	L	L	R	L	R	Swing
10L	L	R	R	L	R	L	L	R	R	L	R	L	
11R	R	L	R	L	R	R	L	R	L	R	L	L	Double Paradiddle
11L	L	R	L	R	L	L	R	L	R	L	R	R	
12R	R	L	R	R	L	R	L	R	L	L	R	L	Double Paradiddle Permutation-DPP1
12L	L	R	L	L	R	L	R	L	R	R	L	R	
13R	R	R	L	R	L	R	L	L	R	L	R	L	DPP2
13L	L	L	R	L	R	L	R	R	L	R	L	R	
14R	R	L	R	L	R	L	L	R	L	R	L	R	DPP3
14L	L	R	L	R	L	R	R	L	R	L	R	L	
15R	R	L	L	R	L	R	L	R	R	L	R	L	DPP4
15L	L	R	R	L	R	L	R	L	L	R	L	R	
16R	R	L	R	R	L	R	L	L	R	L	R	R	Single Paradiddle (X)*
16L	L	R	L	L	R	L	R	R	L	R	L	L	

*(X) indicates cross-rhythm groups of 2's or 4's over triplet subdivision.
**Nago is a religious rhythm originally played by the Yoruba people from Nigeria, now used in Haiti.
***Yanvalou is a religious rhythm originated from the Fon people of Dahomey (Benin), now used in Haiti.
(These are the basic simplified drum set stickings relating to the basic cowbell/ogan [Haitian bell] melodies for Nago and Yanvalou rhythms. The full rhythms are usually played by three or more players and are much more complex.)

Advanced students can take the R's of one sticking and assign it to a limb, and take the L's of another sticking and assign it to another limb, and simultaneously play those stickings over an ostinato. For example, we can assign the R of the Afro-Cuban 6/8 Bell sticking (7R) to the right hand, and play that against the left hand part of the Open Drag sticking (5R) assigned to the left hand over one of the triplet foot ostinatos (found later in the book).

CHAPTER 7
Sticking Page Applications
(Exercises Using the Sticking Matrix Pages in Duplet and Triplet Meter)

All stickings can be played straight, swung, or in between. Please listen to the following players and their mastery of stickings and feel: Buddy Rich, Clyde Stubblefield, Elvin Jones, Tony Williams, Jack DeJohnette, Bill Cobham, Dennis Chambers, Changuito, Tony Allen, Ginger Baker, Questlove, J Dilla, Jojo Mayer, Chris Dave, etc. Listen to as much music and as many different styles as possible and cross-reference the Musical Checklist (The Seven Principles, page 12) as often as possible.

 Tip: If you practice playing these exercises softly, you will be able to play them in all dynamic ranges. If you only practice loudly, you cannot necessarily execute the exercises in a multitude of dynamic ranges.

THE RIGHT HAND LEAD METHOD

In the right hand lead method, you will play the stickings while aligning your right hand with your right foot. Although you will be starting stickings with both the right hand and left hand, the right hand is leading in a melodic fashion. Play the left hand softer so the right hand melody is more prominent.

The following exercises are derived from the duplet meter and triplet meter matrices shown on pages 71–72. Practice with a metronome. Start at 35 BPM and go to 250 BPM. Please play all of the examples from soft to loud. You can create your own charts and exercises by studying the matrix and how it relates to the following exercises.

In the following examples:

R = RH on   a) Cowbell high
                  b) Ride Cymbal
                  c) X-Hat to the right
     and RF (on Bass Drum)

and:

L = LH on   a) Snares off
                 b) Snare cross-stick

Duplet Meter, RH Lead

9R

9L

10R

10L

11R

11L

12R

12L

13R

13L

14R

14L

15R

15L

16R

16L

Triplet Meter, RH Lead

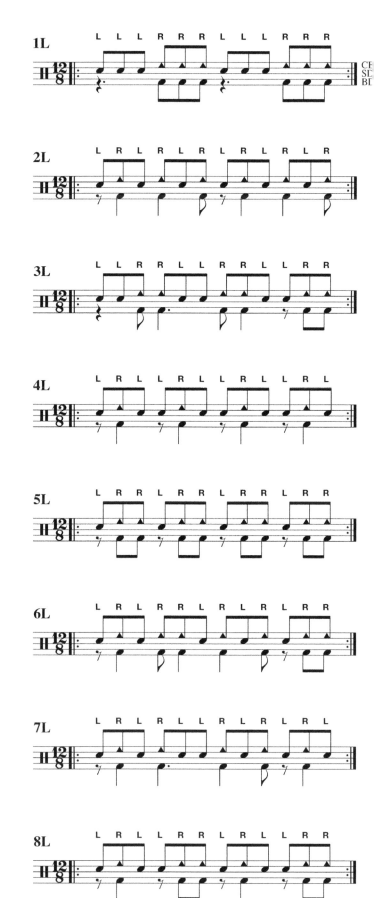

THE LEFT HAND LEAD METHOD

In the left hand lead method, you will play the sticking while aligning your left hand with your right foot. Although you will be starting stickings with both the right hand and left hand, the left hand is leading in a melodic fashion. Play the right hand softer.

The following exercises are also derived from the duplet meter and triplet meter matrices shown on pages 71–72. Practice with the metronome. Start at 35 BPM and go to 250 BPM. Please play all of the examples from soft to loud.

L =	LH on	a) Cowbell low
		b) Hi-Hat to the left
		c) Crash-ride to the left
	and RF (on Bass Drum)	

R =	RH on	a) Snares off
		b) Snare cross-stick

TRACK 40 (0:00–2:00): Duplet Meter, LH Lead: Straight

TRACK 40 (2:02–3:02): Duplet Meter, LH Lead: Swung

Duplet Meter, LH Lead

7R

7L

8R

8L

9R

9L

10R

10L

11R

11L

12R

12L

13R

13L

14R

14L

15R

15L

16R

16L

Triplet Meter, LH Lead

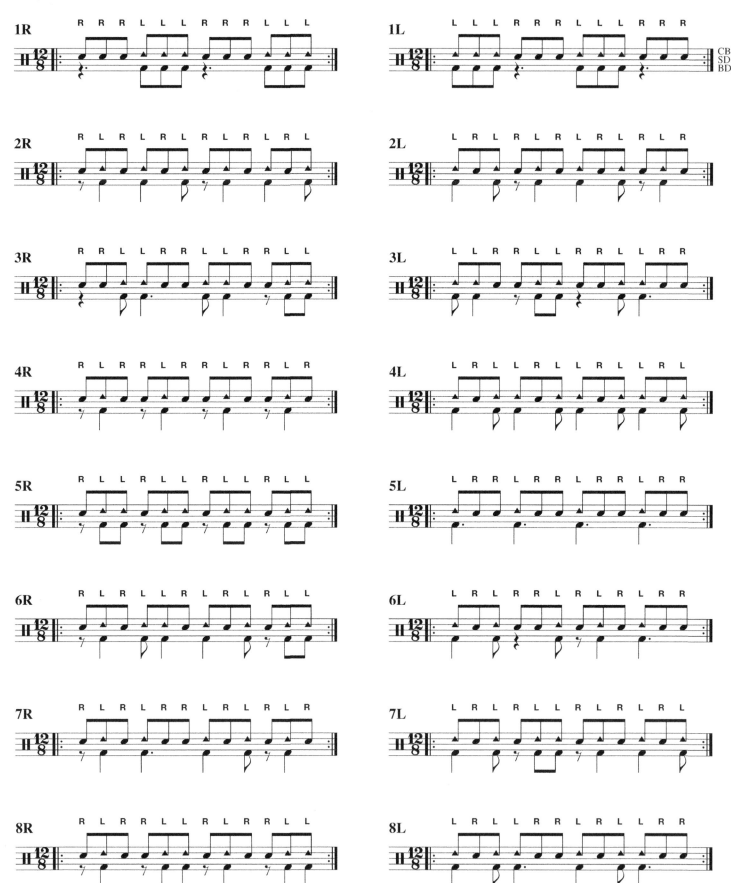

38

THE GHOST STROKE METHOD

Growing up listening to James Brown drummers Clyde Stubblefield and John "Jabo" Starks, and session greats James Gadson, Harvey Mason, Steve Gadd, and Bernard "Pretty" Purdie, and artists like Will Calhoun, Dennis Chambers, Omar Hakim, Kenwood Dennard, and Billy Cobham, I realize there is, was, and always will be something mystical about these drummers.

Besides their impeccable timing, "Pocket," backbeat, foot work, great dynamics, musical setups, and fills, there is also their "time feel" and their use of ghost notes (same as ghost strokes), which add to the individual shades and palettes that each of these great drummers employed.

Ghost notes are super softly played notes (*ppp* to *mp*). You can feel these notes more than you can hear them. Ghost strokes can create a unique flow from a normal sounding beat.

The exercise below (Track 41) is just one example from the matrix on page 71 (5R/5L). Once you have learned this exercise, you can refer to the matrix, take any line from the matrix, and follow the same steps to develop your own ghost stroke beats.

TRACK 41 (0:00–0:20): Ghost Strokes in Duplet Meter, Backbeat on 2 and 4

The backbeat accent is on 3 in duplet meter.

 TRACK 41 (0:21–0:44): Ghost Strokes in Duplet Meter, Backbeat on 3

The exercise below (Track 42) is just one example from the matrix on page 72 (11R/11L). The backbeat accent is on 3 in triplet meter.

 TRACK 42: Ghost Strokes in Triplet Meter, Backbeat on 3

Go through bass drum lines A to D. Play each line four times.

REMEMBER: The prior examples are applications from the sticking matrices in duplet and triplet meter on pages 71–72. Note that you can create your own examples using the other cells in the matrix.

 TRACK 43: Ghost Stroke Drum Solo, Duplet Meter

THE FOOT OSTINATO METHOD

Play through all of the matrix stickings in duplet and triplet meter (pgs. 71–72), either straight or swung, from slow to fast, fast to slow, soft to loud, and loud to soft. Play the softer strokes (*mp*) on the snare and a backbeat accent (*f*) on 2 and 4, or for a half-time feel, play the back accent on beat 3 (*f*) over the following foot ostinatos:

Duplet Stickings/Duplet Matrix Exercise

1. **Four-on-the-Floor (RF = Bass drum on all quarter notes)**
   Hi-Hat LF Ostinatos:
   a) Quarter notes
   b) Eighth notes
   c) Eighth notes with quarter note splash

 TRACK 44 (0:00–0:28): Four-on-the-Floor, Duplet Meter, Backbeat on 2 and 4: Straight

TRACK 44 (0:29–0:55): Four-on-the-Floor, Duplet Meter, Backbeat on 3: Straight

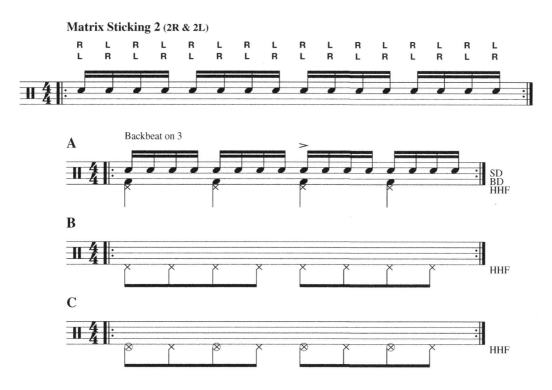

2. Samba-Funk on RF

Hi-Hat LF Ostinatos:
   a) Quarter notes
   b) Eighth notes
   c) Eighth notes with quarter note splash

TRACK 45 (0:00–0:18): Samba-Funk, Duplet Meter, Backbeat on 2 and 4: Straight

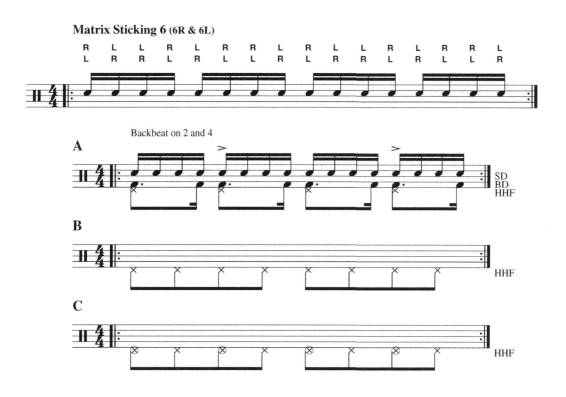

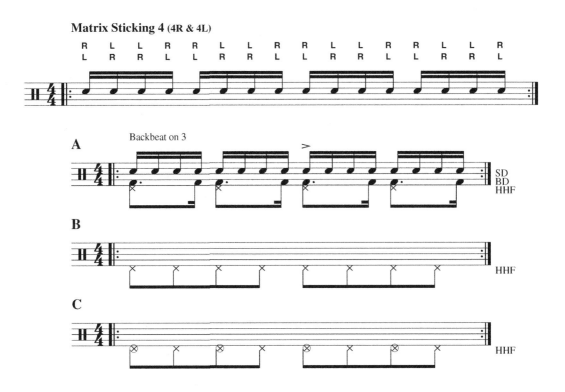

3. Baião/Dance Hall on RF

Hi-Hat LF Ostinatos:
  a) Quarter notes
  b) Eighth notes
  c) Eighth notes with quarter note splash

TRACK 46 (0:00–0:21): Baião/Dance Hall, Duplet Meter, Backbeat on 2 and 4: Straight

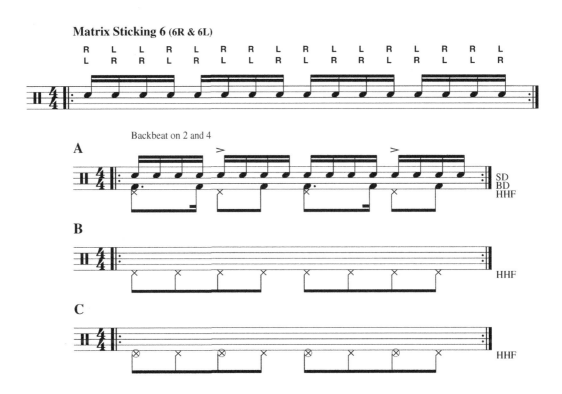

Matrix Sticking 6 (6R & 6L)

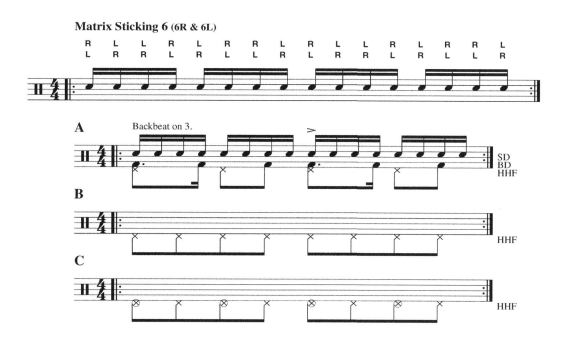

Triplet Stickings/Triplet Matrix Exercise

1. **Four-on-the-Floor (RF = Bass drum on all dotted quarter notes)**

   Hi-Hat LF Ostinatos:
   a) Dotted quarter note
   b) Quarter note
   c) Dotted quarter note splash
   d) Quarter note alternating between splash and closed

🔊 **TRACK 47** (0:00–0:22): Four-on-the-Floor, Triplet Meter, Backbeat on 2 and 4

Matrix Sticking 1 (1R & 1L)

2. Shuffle Bass Drum (RF = Bass drum on first and last of each triplet)

Hi-Hat LF Ostinatos:

    a) Dotted quarter note

    b) Unison with RF shuffle

TRACK 48 (0:00–0:12): Shuffle Bass Drum, Triplet Meter, Backbeat on 2 and 4

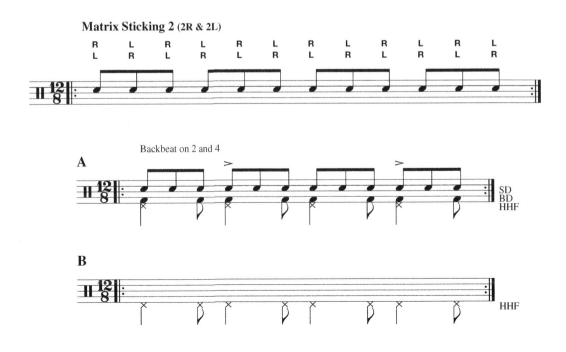

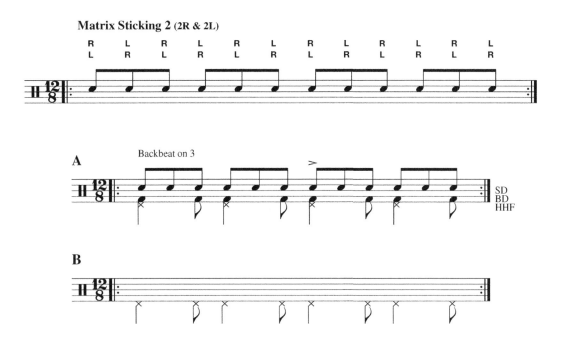

LINEAR STICKING EXERCISES—OFF-BEAT BOUNCE

In this linear section, we play one limb at a time. Please always count out loud when playing these exercises.

The concept here is to play the duplet stickings while adding one, then two, then three hi-hat notes in between them, respectively. In this case, we are using Sticking #10, L&R, from the sticking matrix on page 71. We will play these in both cross-over and open-handed fashion.

Cross-Over:

       R = RF (Bass Drum)
       L = LH (Snare Drum)

       The right hand is on the hi-hat.

Open Handed:

       R = RF (Bass Drum)
       L = RH (Snare Drum)

       The left hand is on the hi-hat.

1. One 32nd note off-beat on closed hi-hat, x-hi-hat, cowbell, or ride

2. Two 32nd note triplet off-beats on closed hi-hat, x-hi-hat, cowbell, or ride

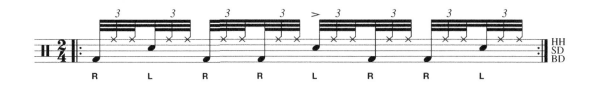

3. Three 64th note off-beats on closed hi-hat, x-hi-hat, cowbell, or ride

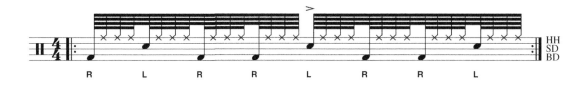

TRACK 49 (0:00–0:16): One 32nd Note Off-Beat

TRACK 49 (0:16–0:30): Two 32nd Note Triplet Off-Beats

TRACK 49 (0:30–0:50): Three 64th Note Off-Beats

COWBELL/HI-HAT/RIDE CYMBAL OSTINATOS

Play the following duplet ostinatos with your right hand on the cowbell, hi-hat, or ride cymbal:

TRACK 50: Duplet Ostinatos

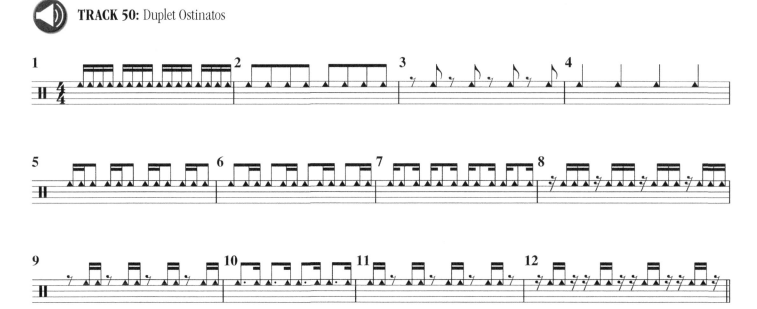

Now while the right hand plays the first ostinato (sixteenth notes), go to the Matrix on page 71 and play sticking 12R applying the R to the right foot on the bass drum, and the L to the left hand on the snare drum. You are dividing the sticking between your right foot and left hand. Also play this reversed, with the left hand playing the ostinato and the right hand on the snare. Now the sticking is divided between the right hand and right foot.

Here is an example of this applied with the Dance Hall 1 sticking (12R):

 TRACK 51: RH Lead

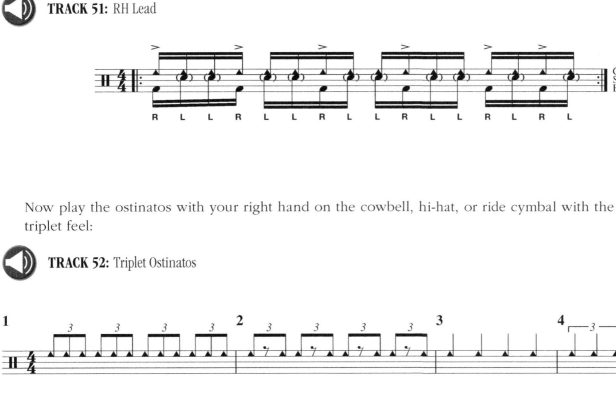

Now play the ostinatos with your right hand on the cowbell, hi-hat, or ride cymbal with the triplet feel:

 TRACK 52: Triplet Ostinatos

Now, while the right hand plays the third ostinato from the music example above (quarter notes), go to the Matrix on page 72, and use 1R (Power of 3 sticking) to play the right foot on the bass drum and the left hand on the snare drum. Again, you are dividing the sticking between your right foot and left hand.

 TRACK 53: Power of 3

Also play this with the left hand playing the ostinato and the right hand on the snare.

Go to the Matrix on page 72 and try this with the Afro-Cuban 6/8 Bell sticking pattern (7R & 7L) against the first ostinato (eighth note triplet) on page 49.

TRACK 54

Also apply it with the left hand playing the ostinato and the right hand playing snare.

Now try this with sticking 3R (from the Matrix on page 72) against ostinato #7, the traditional jazz ride cymbal pattern, on page 49.

TRACK 55

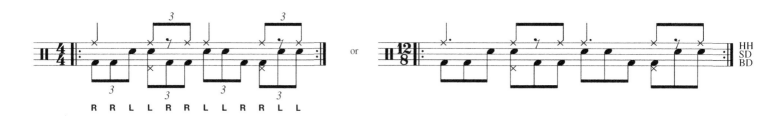

Also apply it with the left hand playing the ostinato and the right hand playing snare.

TRACK 56
TRACK 57: Funky Freestyle 1
TRACK 58: Funky Freestyle 2

THE HARMONIC TOP BOTTOM UNISON METHOD

When we play two or more limbs at the same time, this is known as unison or double stop.

T = Top (Hands):
> *and*

R = **T** = RH and LH together

B = Bottom (Feet):
> *and*

L = **B** = RF and LF together

Play the following unison exercises. Focus on aligning your right hand with your left hand, and your right foot with your left foot. The first applies sticking #7 (PP2) in the duplet matrix; the second applies sticking #8 (Nago) in the triplet matrix.

 TRACK 59: Harmonic Top and Bottom Duplet

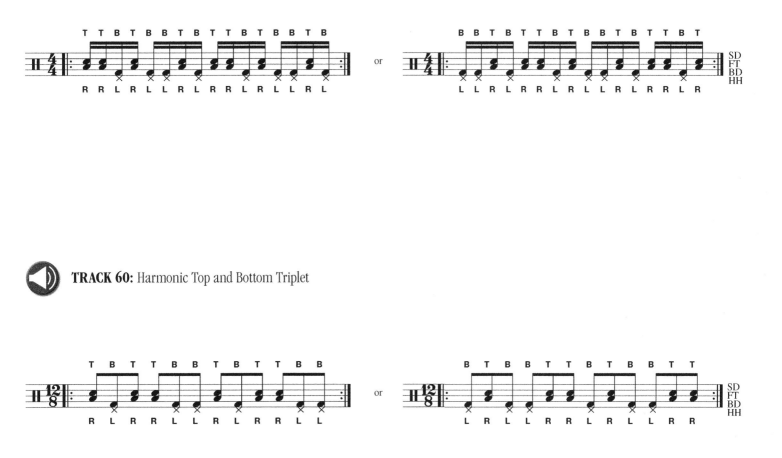

TRACK 60: Harmonic Top and Bottom Triplet

THE SWISS CHRIS SHADOW METHOD

To "shadow it" means to play a note after a previous note. As a shadow for the first example below, you are playing R L R L, which results in R RF L LF R RF L LF. The examples below all reference the sticking matrices on pages 71 and 72.

1. **After each R (RH), "shadow it" with the RF on the bass drum. After each L (LH), "shadow it" with the LF on the hi-hat.**

Duplet Sticking 8: PP3

 TRACK 61

Now try it in the form of a shuffle.

Triplet Sticking 4: Shuffle

 **TRACK 62**

2. **After each R (RH) and L (LH), "shadow it" with the RF on the bass drum.**

Duplet Sticking 11: Rumba Clave 3:2

TRACK 63

Now try it in the form of an open drag triplet.

Triplet Sticking 5: Open Drag

TRACK 64

3. **After each R (RH) and L (LH), "shadow it" with the LF on the hi-hat.**

Apply this coordination with the Dance Hall 1 sticking.

Duplet Sticking 12: Dance Hall 1

TRACK 65

Now try it in an Afro-Cuban clave triplet form.

Triplet Sticking 6: Afro-Cuban 6/8 Clave

TRACK 66

4. **After each R (RH) and L (LH), "shadow it" with two notes with the RF on the bass drum.**

Try this with the Dance Hall 2 sticking.

Duplet Sticking 13: Dance Hall 2

 **TRACK 67**

Now try it in a Yanvalou Triplet form.

Triplet Sticking 9: Yanvalou

 TRACK 68

CHAPTER 8
Melodic Accent Control Charts
(Duplet 8/Duplet 16/Triplet 12)

1. Read each melodic letter in all three charts below 20 times. (Count and clap the attack of the accent.)

2. Clap on 2 and 4, and sing the note making sure you are singing the length of the note. This is very important. Some drummers only think of the attack, not the duration of the note.

3. Orchestrate this on the drums. Play each melodic letter four times. Apply the long notes onto the crash, open hi-hat, or ride. Layer it with a kick. Play the short notes on the snare or toms.

4. Play:
   three bars of groove, one bar of the Melodic Accent letter
   seven bars of groove, one bar of the Melodic Accent letter

TRACK 69: Duplet 8, Count and Clap

TRACK 70: Duplet 8, Clap and Sing

TRACK 71: Duplet 8, Orchestrate (played four times)

TRACK 72: Duplet 8; Three Bars of Groove, One Bar of Melodic Accent

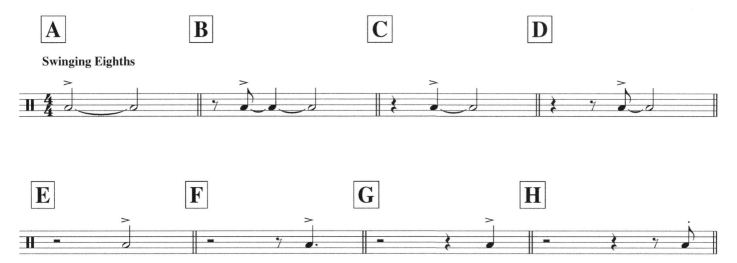

TRACK 73: Duplet 16, Count and Clap

TRACK 74: Duplet 16, Clap and Sing

TRACK 75: Freestyle Duplet 16

TRACK 76: Duplet 16; Three Bars of Groove, One Bar of Melodic Accent

TRACK 77: Duplet 16; Seven Bars of Groove, One Bar of Melodic Accent

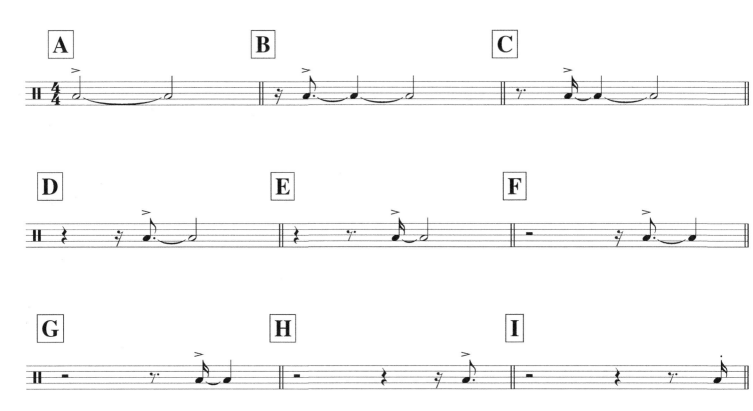

TRACK 78: Triplet 12, Count and Clap

TRACK 79: Triplet 12, Clap and Sing

TRACK 80: Freestyle Triplet Meter Interlude

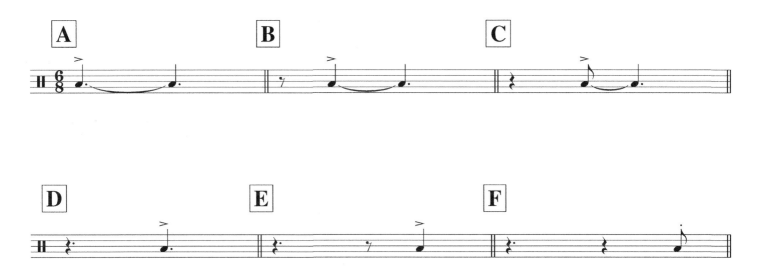

CHAPTER 9
The Flam Rudiment

A traditional flam is a rudiment consisting of a quiet "grace" note on one hand, right before a louder primary stroke on the opposite hand. The two notes are played almost simultaneously and are intended to sound like a single broader note.

Traditional Flam

 **TRACK 81**

But there are also the following variations:

Open Flam

Open flams have a more loose, sloppy feel.

 TRACK 81

The "o" above the grace note is the notational marking for the open flam.

Reversed Flam (Malf)

The grace note follows the main stroke.

 **TRACK 81**

Reversed Open Flam (Malf)

Reversed open flams are played the same as the reversed flam, but with a more loose feel.

 TRACK 82

Broken Flam

The broken flam can be played either traditional or open, and the flam is divided up on your kit.

 TRACK 82

CHAPTER 10
"Making Swiss Cheese"
(The Four Gears)

This section is dedicated to Clifford Wesley, an amazing drummer and educator.

Choose your sticking from the duplet sticking matrix and add accents.

Gear 1: Paradiddle

TRACK 82

Add the flam to the accents.

Gear 2: Flamadiddle

TRACK 82

Leave out the flam and add a drag to the accents.

Gear 3: Dragadiddle

TRACK 82

Add both the flam and the drag to the accents and you have Swiss Cheese!

Gear 4: Cheeseadiddle

TRACK 82

CHAPTER 11
The Swiss Chris Flam Shadow

Go to The Swiss Chris Shadow Method (page 52) and replace single hits R and L with flams (R = RH flam and L = LH flam). Also play the sticking matrices with the following applications.

a. "Shadow it" with RF on the bass drum.

b. "Shadow it" with LF on the hi-hat.

c. "Shadow it" with two notes using the RF on the bass drum.

TRACK 83: Duplet Meter, Sticking 8

TRACK 84: Triplet Meter, Sticking 4

TRACK 85: Triplet Meter, Sticking 5; RF Shadow

TRACK 86: Duplet Meter, Sticking 12; RF Shadow

TRACK 87: Triplet Meter, Sticking 6; LF Shadow

TRACK 88: Duplet Meter, Sticking 13; RF Shadow

TRACK 89: Triplet Meter, Sticking 9; RF Double

CHAPTER 12
Basic Polyrhythms

3 over 2

 TRACK 90 (0:00–0:10)

2 over 3

 TRACK 90 (0:11–0:18)

4 over 3

 TRACK 90 (0:18–0:29)

3 over 4

 TRACK 90 (0:29–0:44)

 TRACK 90 (0:45–1:30): Musical Applications

TRACK 91: Ending Freestyle Triplet Meter

TRACK 92: Swiss GoGo Freestyle

TRACK 93: 12/8 Give Thanks

TRACK 94: Peace Out

MUSIC RECOMMENDATIONS

DRUMMER	RECORD TITLE OR SONG	ARTIST
Babatunde Olatunji	*Drums of Passion*	Olatunji
Bonga Gaston Jean-Baptiste	*Kanzo*	Bonga
Bonga and the Vodou Drums	*Ayiti Afrika*	Bonga & Vodou Drums
Various Artists	*Angels in the Mirror*	Vodou Music of Haiti
Frisner Augustin	*Drums of Vodou*	Frisner Augustin
Various Drummers	*Vodou Adjae*	Boukman Eksperyans
Various Drummers	*Pale Avem*	Rara Machine
Tito Puente	*La Leyenda*	Tito Puente
Tito Puente	*Top Percussion*	Tito Puente
Changuito	Any or all recordings	Los Van Van
Baby Dodds	*The King Oliver Creole Jazz Band 1923 Featuring Louis Armstrong*	King Oliver
Ginger Baker & Tony Allen	*Live!*	Fela Ransome-Kuti and the Africa '70
Tony Allen	All Fela recordings	Fela
Bernard "Pretty" Purdie	*The Revolution Will Not Be Televised*	Gil Scott-Heron
Nilaja Obabi	*The Last Poets*	The Last Poets
Max Roach	"Caravan"	Clifford Brown & Max Roach
Max Roach	*We Insist!*	Abbey Lincoln & Max Roach
Elvin Jones	*A Love Supreme*	John Coltrane
Elvin Jones	*Speak No Evil*	Wayne Shorter
Tony Williams	*Four & More*	Miles Davis
Tony Williams	*Seven Steps to Heaven*	Miles Davis
Bob Moses	*Bright Size Life*	Pat Metheny
Bill Cobham	*The Best of Billy Cobham*	Bill Cobham
Bill Cobham	*Crosswinds*	Bill Cobham
Bill Cobham	*Spectrum*	Bill Cobham
Clyde Stubblefield	*In the Jungle Groove*	James Brown
Clyde Stubblefield	"Cold Sweat"	James Brown
Clyde Stubblefield	"Give It Up or Turnit a Loose" (Live)	James Brown
John "Jabo" Starks	"I Know You Got Soul"	Bobby Bird
Bernard "Pretty" Purdie	"Rock Steady"	Aretha Franklin
Robbie McIntosh	"Pick Up the Pieces"	Average White Band
George Brown	*Best of Kool & the Gang*	Kool & the Gang
James "Diamond" Williams	*Best of the Ohio Players*	Ohio Players

David Garibaldi	*Best of Tower of Power*	Tower of Power
Mike Clark	"Actual Proof"	Herbie Hancock
Kenwood Dennard	*Life on Planet Groove*	Maceo Parker
C. Will (Courtney Williams)	"Perfection" (Raising Hell)	Run-DMC
Errol Bedward (Pumpkin)	"Feel the Heartbeat"	Treacherous Three
Errol Bedward (Pumpkin)	"Move to the Groove"	Disco Four
Harvey Mason	*Head Hunters*	Herbie Hancock
Keith Leblanc	"Rapper's Delight"	Sugarhill Gang
Keith Leblanc	"The Message"/"Freedom"	Grandmaster Flash/Melle Mel
Dennis Chambers	*Live at the Beverly Theatre in Hollywood*	P-Funk All Stars
Dennis Chambers	*Blue Matter*	John Scofield
Ricky Wellman	*Go Go Swing Live*	Chuck Brown & The Soul Searchers
Emmett Nixon	*Trouble Funk Live*	Trouble Funk
Questlove (Ahmir-Khalib Thompson)	*Do You Want More?!!!??!*	The Roots
Questlove (Ahmir-Khalib Thompson	Any Recording	Any Artist
Gene Lake	*Peace Beyond Passion*	Me'Shell NdegeOcello
Jeff Porcaro	*Toto*	Toto
Jeff Porcaro	"Thriller"	Michael Jackson
Chris "Daddy" Dave	*Definition of a Band*	Mint Condition
Chris "Daddy" Dave	*Double Booked*	Robert Glasper
Chris "Daddy" Dave	*Mary*	Mary J. Blige
Will Calhoun	*Time's Up/Vivid/Stain*	Living Colour
Will Calhoun	Any Recording	Will Calhoun
J Dilla	*Fantastic 1*	Slum Village
J Dilla	Any Recording	Any Artist
Swiss Chris Flueck	*Get Lifted*	John Legend
Swiss Chris Flueck	*Once Again*	John Legend
Swiss Chris Flueck	*Stand Out*	Ladell McLin
Don Guillaume	*Masquerade*	Wyclef Jean
"Spanky" McCurdy	*Justified*	Justin Timberlake
"Spanky" McCurdy	*Luvanmusiq*	Musiq Soulchild
Marvin McQuitty	*Pages of Life: Chapters 1 & 2*	Fred Hammond
Aaron Spears	*Confessions*	Usher
Marvin "Smitty" Smith	*Extensions*	Dave Holland
Stevie Wonder	*Song in the Key of Life*	Stevie Wonder
Jeff "Lo" Davis	*Now That I'm Here*	Beverly Crawford
Billy Hart	*Crossings*	Herbie Hancock

ADDITIONAL BOOK RECOMMENDATIONS

Drumopedia by Dan Britt

Drumset for Beginners by Paul Hose and Jim Farey

Contemporary Drumset Phrasing by Frank Katz

World Fusion Drumming by Skip Hadden

The Art of Modern Jazz Drumming by Jack DeJohnette and Charlie Perry

Funk Drumming by Mike Clark/Transcription by Towner Galaher

The Commandments of Early Rhythm and Blues Drumming by Zoro and Daniel Glass

The Commandments of R&B Drumming by Zoro w/Russ Miller/Transcription and Notation by Brian Mason

Universal Rhythms for Drumset by Dave DiCenso

Advanced Funk Studies by Rick Latham

It's About Time by Fred Dinkins

Open-Handed Playing Vol. 1 by Claus Hessler w/Dom Famularo

The New Breed by Gary Chester

West African Rhythms for Drumset by Royal Hartigan with Abraham Adzenyah and Freeman Donkor

Advanced Concepts by Kim Plainfield

4-Way Coordination by Marvin Dahlgren and Elliot Fine

The Art of Playing Timbales by Victor Rendon

Conversations in Clave by Horacio "El Negro" Hernandez

The Breakbeat Bible by Mike Adamo

Drumming with the Mambo King by Tito Puente and Jim Payne

Studio and Big Band Drumming by Steve Houghton

Steve Gadd Up Close by Steve Gadd and Bobby Cleall

Riddim: Claves of African Origin by Billy Martin/Edited by Dan Thress

The Beat, The Body, & The Brain II by Skip Hadden

Let It Flow by Omar Hakim

Rhythmic Accents by Paul Cellucci

The Rhythm Library System by Gordy Knudtson

Stickings and Orchestrations for Drum Set by Casey Scheuerell

Serious Moves by Dennis Chambers

In the Pocket by Dennis Chambers

The Art of Drumming by Robert Kaufman

Drum Wisdom by Bob Moses

Rudimental Jazz: Musical Application of Rudiments to the Drum Set by Joe Morello

All of Gary Chaffee's books and DVDs

INSPIRATIONAL QUOTES

"Give thanks" for the drums. What a

blessing and an opportunity it is to play, learn,

and constantly grow

as a musician and human

in this time and space…

constantly expanding…"

—Swiss Chris

"No one else can dance your dance, sing your song.

Never compete with anybody…just grow…you can

learn something from everybody."

—Swiss Chris

"Each one, teach one."

—African Proverb

"Consistent practice of music opens the inner pathways

to channel the infinite sounds of the universe."

—Alexander Adhami, Multi-Instrumentalist

"Inspire to aspire, aspire to inspire."

—Dom Famularo, Educator/Drummer

"Just advance."

—Kenwood Dennard, Educator/Drummer

"The drum does not lie, it speaks the truth.

It is air traveling through a cylinder

before, on, or after the heartbeat, soft to loud."

—Swiss Chris

ACKNOWLEDGMENTS

Give thanks to everybody involved supporting this fun project. First and foremost, thanks to everybody at **Cherry Lane Music**, especially **Peter W. Primont**, **John Stix**, **Mark Phillips**, and **Susan Poliniak**. Additional thanks to **Jackie Muth** at **Hal Leonard Corporation**.

Special thanks go out to the patient, super-talented **Mr. Dan Britt** for helping in the production process of the written part of this book … Give thanks for your endless support … Dan Britt rocks … !!

Big thanks to all the great **musicians and friends** out there from the past, present, and future … too many spirits and souls to mention …

Also give thanks to my father **Ulrich Flueck and family**, to my brother **Thomas Flueck and family**, and to my cousin **J.J. Flueck and family**.

Super special thanks to my beautiful, strong, and patient wife **Lakecia Davis-Flueck**.

Special thanks to all of my sponsors:

Sabian (Robert Zildjian, Paul Cellucci, Christian Stankee, Ann McNally, Christian Koch, Shirlene Lau, and Stephen Lawson)

Regal Tip/Calato (Joe Calato, Carol Calato, and Michelle Calato)

Natal Drums (Paul Marshall, Craig Glover, Dendy Jarrett, Paul Hose, Jason Roper, and Gary Walmsley)

Roland (Tim Root, Steve Fisher, and Bob Duncan)

Evans (Marco Soccoli, Jenifer Tooke)

Beat Kangz Electronics (Michael Crabtree, Aja Emmanuel, Reavis Mitchell, and Nadir Omowale), "Da Beat Thang Rules"

Everybody at **Hansenfutz Footpedals**, **Alesis/Akai Electronics**, **CAD Mics**, **Apple**, **Ableton**, and **Propellerhead Software** for providing me with superior instruments for this occasion.

Give thanks to all my drum teachers/mentors:

Jakob Otter (Tambourenverein Laupersdorf, Switzerland)

Norbert Lehmann (Dante Agostini, Olten, Switzerland)

Felix Knusel (Kantonsschule Zofingen, Switzerland)

All my teachers at **Berklee School of Music**, Boston, USA:

Ron Savage, Casey Scheuerell, Skip Hadden, Joanne Brackeen, Ed Uribe, Giovanni Hidalgo, Victor Mendoza, Ian Froman, Joe Hunt, Ed Kaspik, and everybody I forgot to mention…

Kenwood Dennard (Mentor/Teacher), **Bob Moses** (NEC Boston/Teacher), **Johnny Vidacovich** (Teacher), **Marvin "Smitty" Smith** (Teacher), **Joe Heredia** (Master Class), **Jojo Mayer** (Master Class), **Alan Dawson** (Teacher), **Jim Chapin** (Teacher), **Joe Morello** (Teacher), **Lenny Nelson** (Teacher), **Dr. Brian Willson** (Mentor/Teacher), **"Pops" Dennis Davis** (Mentor), **Dom Famularo** (Mentor/Teacher), **Steve Smith** (Master Class), **Cliff Wesley** (Teacher/Mentor), **Morris "Arnie" Lang** (Mentor/Teacher)

Thanks to **Frank Khatz** (Teacher, Collective NYC), **Kim Plainfield** (Teacher, Collective NYC), **"Merci beaucoup" Bonga Gaston Jean-Baptiste** (Haitian Drum Teacher/Mentor)

Also special thanks to artists/producers who influenced me and my playing:

Louis Armstrong, Baby Dodds, Buddy Rich, Gene Krupa, Louis Bellson, Lionel Hampton, Miles Davis, John Coltrane, Charlie Parker, Dizzy Gillespie, Charles Mingus, Jimmy Cobb, Art Blakey, Hani Ali, Papa Joe Jones, Philly Joe Jones, Max Roach, Elvin Jones, Ed Thigpen, Roy Haynes, Tony Williams, Jack DeJohnette, Questlove (Ahmir-Khalib Thompson), Keith LeBlanc, Dennis Chambers, Steve Jordan, Stevie Wonder, Jerry Wonda, Chris "Daddy" Dave, Deantoni Parks, Dr. Roger Linn, Han Bennink, Pierre Favre, Daniel Humair, Andy Brugger, Dannie Richmond, Al Foster, Phil Collins, Chester Thompson, Manu Katché, Buddy Miles, Billy Cox, Jimi Hendrix, Peter Erskine, Jeff Queen, Jeff Porcaro, Jeff "Tain" Watts, Mark Mondesir, Thomas Lang, Tomas Haake, Stewart Copeland, the X-Ecutioners, J Dilla, Scott La Rock, Pete Rock, Pumpkin (The King of The Beats), Run-DMC, Doug E. Fresh, Slick Rick, Mos Def, Talib Kweli, Chubb Rock, Kid Lucky, Bobby and Taylor McFerrin, Zulu Nation, Rock Steady Crew, Lyricist Lounge, Fat Beats, Wyclef Jean, Poet Tree, Scratch, Sonny Emory, Aaron Spears, "Spanky" McCurdy, Todd Snare, Clyde Stubblefield, John "Jabo" Starks, Bernard "Pretty" Purdie, Al Jackson Jr., James "Diamond" Williams, David Garibaldi, Ricky Lawson, Eddie Harris, James Brown, Prince, Jose Luis "Changuito" Quintana, Michael Jackson, Sir Elton John, Kanye West, Jay-Z, Biggie Smalls, Tupac Shakur, Big L, D'Angelo, Maxwell, John Legend, Devo Springsteen, Fela Kuti, Los Van Van, The Last Poets, Jay Rodriguez, Chris Theberge, Groove Collection, Gil Scott-Heron, Poor Righteous Teachers, Eminem, Bajah and the Dry Eye Crew, The Roots, Wu-Tang, Public Enemy, Cypress Hill, Ladell McLin, James "Blood" Ulmer, Ornette Coleman, Sun Ra, Burnt Sugar, Living Colour, Herbie Hancock, Keith Jarrett, Joanne Brackeen, Alexander Adhami, Adonis Rose, Blitz the Ambassador, Marc Gilmore, John Roberts, John Blackwell, Abe Laboriel Sr. and Jr., Poogie Bell, Adam Deitch, Steve Gadd, Omar Hakim, Harvey Mason, Ndugu Chancler, Gerry Brown, Mike Clark, Steve Houghton, Sly Dunbar, Larry McDonald, Tony Royster Jr., Ronald Bruner Jr., Stanton Moore, Will Calhoun, Ginger Baker, Tony Allen, Jeff "Lo" Davis, Chesney Snow, Rahzel, Immortal Technique, Kenny Muhammad, Alonzo Harris, Gogo Godson, Mazzi with S.O.U.L. Purpose, Akim Funk Buddha, Princess Lockeroo, Sidney Mills, Steel Pulse, Anthony Mouzon, Sanford Biggers and Moon Medicine, Mark Hines and The Marksmen, Eric "Vietnam" Sadler, Lex Salder, Gloria Gaynor, and Divinity Roxx … and on and on … everybody. (The insects were the first musicians on this planet.)

This book is dedicated to my late mother, **Erika Flueck-Roschi**, and to the late **Mr. Jim Chapin** (Educator/Drummer).

Recording Credits:

Drum Tracking/Programming at SwissChris777 LAB East Flatbush, Brooklyn
Additional Overdubs and Mixing at Music Works NYC, Upper West Side
Mastering at Hummingbird Music, NYC

Tracking Engineer/Programmer: **Josh Ortiz**
Mix Engineer: **Eli Zarama**
Mastering Engineer: **Christos Tsantilis**
Supervising Producer: **Chris Theberge**
Special thanks to **Surya Botofasina**: Keyboards
Special thanks to the funky Brooklyn brothers, **Aaron** and **Josh "Sway" Guillen**

Give thanks to **Scott Meszaros** for connecting the "Deal."

"Energy can never be created or destroyed, everything

is energy all connected in, through, or out of form, we are

spiritual beings … We are an energy field in a larger energy field."

ABOUT THE AUTHOR

Swiss Chris is an in-demand first-call session drummer/music director. He recently worked with the legendary Gloria Gaynor doing TV appearances and touring for the 30th anniversary "I Will Survive" promo. Swiss is well-known for his work as musical director and drummer for the nine-time GRAMMY® winner John Legend, with whom he worked for four years. He is now concentrating on his own solo career with a forthcoming album. Swiss is also actively involved with his charitable organization, S.W.I.S.S. (Saving With Instruments, Samples and Soundz), dedicated to healing, education, and promoting communication through music for the betterment of the world.

During his tenure with John Legend, Swiss's unique style was exposed to worldwide audiences—he performed all over the world with numerous tours both in the U.S. and abroad. Swiss performed on John Legend's first two albums, *Get Lifted* (three GRAMMYs) and *Once Again* (two GRAMMYs). In detail, Swiss played on the GRAMMY Award-winning hit "So High" (*Get Lifted*) and on the hit single "Save Room" (*Once Again*). In addition to that, he recorded on the John Legend "So High" (Cloud 9 remix) featuring Miss Lauryn Hill.

Also, two classic DVDs were recorded: *John Legend: Live at the House of Blues* and *John Legend: Live from Philadelphia*.

While working with John Legend, Swiss Chris had the pleasure of being able to work with artists like Sir Elton John, Kanye West, Snoop Dogg, India Arie, Common, Wyclef Jean, DJ Dummy, DJ A-Trak, Corinne Bailey Rae, and many more.

Swiss Chris was also the musical director/drummer for the HomeSchool Records/Bailey's sponsored Tour 2008 and video featuring "Estelle" Fanta Swaray.

Swiss is currently working with Ladell McLin, the Afro hip-hop group Bajah and the Dry Eye Crew, Zimbabwe Legit, Mazzi with S.O.U.L. Purpose, and his own group, The Dream Team One (Swiss Chris Freestyle Shows).

Swiss Chris stars in the hip-hop/rock video with Talib Kweli's group, Idle Warship, on the track "Black Snake Moan."

He also recently recorded with the world famous drummer Billy Cobham, DMC, and Chuck D. from Public Enemy.

Coming to New York via Boston, Swiss worked with a local funk band led by the Jewish James Brown, Milo Z. He also worked with hip-hop old school legends like Chubb Rock, Charlie Brown from Leaders of the New School, Slick Rick, Grandmaster Caz, the Rock Steady Crew, and DJ Johnny Juice from Public Enemy.

While in the States, Swiss Chris earned his bachelor's degree in performance from the Berklee School of Music in Boston, Massachusetts. He further studied at Drummers Collective in New York. He received multiple awards and honors as a marching band field drummer, and as a big band and contemporary jazz drummer in Switzerland.

Swiss has studied with diverse teachers such as Bob Moses, Marvin "Smitty" Smith, Kim Plainfield, Frank Katz, Ian Froman, Ron Savage, Casey Scheuerell, Kenwood Dennard, Skip Hadden, Joe Morello, Jim Chapin, and last but not least, the Drumdoctor Dom Famularo.

Swiss has been on BET in a featured performance as the musical director/drummer for the "Ed Gordon Show" with the Last Poets, Jessica Care Moore, and Mums from the hit HBO show "Oz." Swiss performed and/or recorded with conscious MCs like Mos Def, Dead Prez, Acrobatic, Afu-Ra, and Milano.

Swiss was the musical director and house drummer for the legendary Lyricist Lounge. He worked for multiple fundraisers and charity events with the political activist group Earthdriver, and performed at Madison Square Garden for a Mumia Abu-Jamal Benefit.

Swiss Chris was also the musical director/drummer/programmer for Mexicano 777 (featuring KRS-One and Mad Lion) and Bazaar Royale (MTV appearance). He toured Eastern and Western Europe with the legendary James "Blood" Ulmer. He performed at the Apollo Theater with Billy Cox (Jimi Hendrix, Band of Gypsys) and Ladell McLin, Jessica Care Moore, and Imani Uzuri with Burnt Sugar.

Television appearances included MTV's "Video Music Awards," "The Soul Train Music Awards," The Nobel Peace Prize Award Ceremony at Oslo, Jamaican, and Trinidad Festivals, DTV "Royal Albert Hall Show," iTunes, Yahoo, and Verizon Promotional Tours, "The Tyra Banks Show," "Ellen," "The View," "Jimmy Kimmel Live!," "Late Show with David Letterman," "Jools Holland's BBC," "Late Night with Conan O'Brien," "Oprah," "Good Morning America," "MTV Music Awards Japan," "VH1 Super Bowl Pepsi Smash," and "The CBS Early Show," "The Tonight Show with Jay Leno," "BET Gospel," Oxygen Network's "Custom Concert," MTV and GRAMMY appearances in the US, Europe, and MTV Africa, and the "Vibe Festival" with Common and Kanye West.

Swiss Chris endorses Natal Drums, Sabian Cymbals, Regal Tip/Calato Drumsticks, Evans Drumheads, Roland, Hansenfutz Foot Pedals, Alesis/Akai Electronics, CAD Mics, Apple, Ableton, and Propellerhead Software.

Most recently, Swiss served as faculty member for Berklee's Five-Week Summer Performance Program, and performed at Musikmesse Frankfurt for the Drum Company NATAL, at the World Beatbox Championship with Kenny Muhammad and the legendary Rahzel, at the Apollo Soundstage Series, and with legendary rap group Black Moon, Delmar Brown World Pop Experience, and legendary bassist Doug Wimbish.

The Swiss Chris Modern Drum School (Swiss Chris 777 LLC) is located in New York City. For more information about private instruction, visit www.SwissChris777.com.

DRUM NOTATION LEGEND

HI-HAT

OPEN AND CLOSED HI-HAT: Strike the open hi-hat on notes labeled with an o. Strike the closed hi-hat on unlabeled notes.

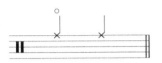

HI-HAT WITH FOOT: Clap hi-hat cymbals together with foot pedal.

HI-HAT WITH SLUR: The open hi-hat is struck and then closed with the foot on the beat indicated by the hi-hat w/foot notation below, creating a *shoop* sound.

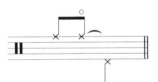

HI-HAT BARK: The open hi-hat is struck and is immediately, almost simultaneously, closed so that the *shoop* sound is severely clipped.

HI-HAT SPLASH: Clash the cymbals together forcibly with your foot, then allow them to ring. This foot splash creates a sound akin to a pair of small crash cymbals.

CYMBALS

CHOKE: Hit the crash cymbal and catch it immediately with the other hand, producing a short, choked crash sound.

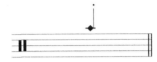

BELL OF CYMBAL: Hit the cymbal near the center, directly on the cup or bell portion.

CYMBAL ROLL: Play a roll on the cymbal rapidly enough to produce a sustained, uninterrupted *shhh* sound lasting for the number of beats indicated.

OTHER PERCUSSION

COWBELLS: Strike the cowbell at the mouth for a loud sound, or on top with the tip of the stick for a lighter, unaccented sound. Multiple-pitch cowbells can be used on a drum set.

DRUMS

CROSS-STICK: Anchor the tip end of the stick on the snare drum skin at the eight o'clock position, two to three inches from the rim. Then raise and lower the butt end, striking the rim at the two o'clock position, producing a clicky, woodblock-type sound.

FLAM: Hit the drum with both sticks, one slightly after the other, producing a single, thick-sounding note.

DRAG/RUFF: Play the grace notes rapidly and as close to the principal note as possible. The grace notes are unaccented and should be played slightly before the beat. The principal note is accented and played directly on the beat.

CLOSED ROLL: Play a roll on the snare drum creating a sustained, uninterrupted *tshhh* sound lasting for the duration of the rhythm indicated and with no break between the two tied notes.

STICKING MATRIX IN DUPLET METER
(BINARY RHYTHM)

1R	R	R	R	R		L	L	L	L		R	R	R	R		L	L	L	L
1L	L	L	L	L		R	R	R	R		L	L	L	L		R	R	R	R
2R	R	L	R	L		R	L	R	L		R	L	R	L		R	L	R	L
2L	L	R	L	R		L	R	L	R		L	R	L	R		L	R	L	R
3R	R	R	L	L		R	R	L	L		R	R	L	L		R	R	L	L
3L	L	L	R	R		L	L	R	R		L	L	R	R		L	L	R	R
4R	R	L	L	R		R	L	L	R		R	L	L	R		R	L	L	R
4L	L	R	R	L		L	R	R	L		L	R	R	L		L	R	R	L
5R	R	L	R	R		L	R	L	L		R	L	R	R		L	R	L	L
5L	L	R	L	L		R	L	R	R		L	R	L	L		R	L	R	R
6R	R	L	L	R		L	R	R	L		R	L	L	R		L	R	R	L
6L	L	R	R	L		R	L	L	R		L	R	R	L		R	L	L	R
7R	R	R	L	R		L	L	R	L		R	R	L	R		L	L	R	L
7L	L	L	R	L		R	R	L	R		L	L	R	L		R	R	L	R
8R	R	L	R	L		L	R	L	R		R	L	R	L		L	R	L	R
8L	L	R	L	R		R	L	R	L		L	R	L	R		R	L	R	L
9R	R	L	R	L		R	L	R	R		L	R	L	R		L	R	L	L
9L	L	R	L	R		L	R	L	L		R	L	R	L		R	L	R	R
10R	R	L	R	R		L	R	R	L		R	L	R	R		L	R	R	L
10L	L	R	L	L		R	L	L	R		L	R	L	L		R	L	L	R
11R	R	L	L	R		L	L	L	R		L	L	R	L		R	L	L	L
11L	L	R	R	L		R	R	R	L		R	R	L	R		L	R	R	R
12R	R	L	L	R		L	L	R	L		L	R	L	L		R	L	R	L
12L	L	R	R	L		R	R	L	R		R	L	R	R		L	R	L	R
13R	R	L	L	R		L	L	R	L		R	L	L	R		L	L	R	L
13L	L	R	R	L		R	R	L	R		L	R	R	L		R	R	L	R
14R	R	L	R	R		L	L	R	L		R	R	L	L		R	L	R	R
14L	L	R	L	L		R	R	L	R		L	L	R	R		L	R	L	L
15R	R	L	L	R		L	L	R	L		L	R	L	L		R	L	R	R
15L	L	R	R	L		R	R	L	R		R	L	R	R		L	R	L	L
16R	R	L	R	R		R	R	L	R		L	L	L	L		R	L	R	R
16L	L	R	L	L		L	L	R	L		R	R	R	R		L	R	L	L

STICKING MATRIX IN TRIPLET METER
(TERNARY RHYTHM)

1R	R	R	R	L	L	L	R	R	R	L	L	L
1L	L	L	L	R	R	R	L	L	L	R	R	R
2R	R	L	R	L	R	L	R	L	R	L	R	L
2L	L	R	L	R	L	R	L	R	L	R	L	R
3R	R	R	L	L	R	R	L	L	R	R	L	L
3L	L	L	R	R	L	L	R	R	L	L	R	R
4R	R	L	R	R	L	R	R	L	R	R	L	R
4L	L	R	L	L	R	L	L	R	L	L	R	L
5R	R	L	L	R	L	L	R	L	L	R	L	L
5L	L	R	R	L	R	R	L	R	R	L	R	R
6R	R	L	R	L	L	R	L	R	L	R	L	L
6L	L	R	L	R	R	L	R	L	R	L	R	R
7R	R	L	R	L	R	R	L	R	L	R	L	R
7L	L	R	L	R	L	L	R	L	R	L	R	L
8R	R	L	R	R	L	L	R	L	R	R	L	L
8L	L	R	L	L	R	R	L	R	L	L	R	R
9R	R	L	R	L	R	L	R	R	L	R	L	R
9L	L	R	L	R	L	R	L	L	R	L	R	L
10R	R	L	L	R	L	R	R	L	L	R	L	R
10L	L	R	R	L	R	L	L	R	R	L	R	L
11R	R	L	R	L	R	R	L	R	L	R	L	L
11L	L	R	L	R	L	L	R	L	R	L	R	R
12R	R	L	R	R	L	R	L	R	L	L	R	L
12L	L	R	L	L	R	L	R	L	R	R	L	R
13R	R	R	L	R	L	R	L	L	R	L	R	L
13L	L	L	R	L	R	L	R	R	L	R	L	R
14R	R	L	R	L	R	L	L	R	L	R	L	R
14L	L	R	L	R	L	R	R	L	R	L	R	L
15R	R	L	L	R	L	R	L	R	R	L	R	L
15L	L	R	R	L	R	L	R	L	L	R	L	R
16R	R	L	R	R	L	R	L	L	R	L	R	R
16L	L	R	L	L	R	L	R	R	L	R	L	L